written and illustrated
by
carolyn stachowski
for
insight on the inside

a generosity practice of

insight meditation
community of washington
DC
IMCW. org

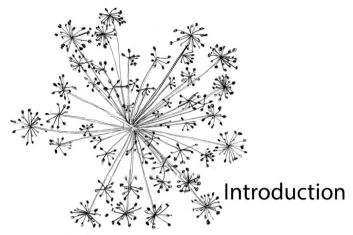

Introduction

The aim of this workbook is to explain ending stress, through the practice of mindfulness, in a simple way.

This practice is a *science:* ideas that we test to find the truth. What follows are ideas and some suggested methods for testing them. In fact, no help can come of these practices unless we test them in our particular life circumstances.

For more than 2,500 years, many people have discovered that this practice leads to an unshakeable peace. Now, our scientists are conducting sophisticated studies confirming that the mindfulness practice is an effective system for training the mind so that we are healthier and happier.

This is not complicated, but practicing is difficult. So, we need to be prepared for what we're up against. Our conditioning drives us toward fearful and dissatisfied states. Yet if we can acknowledge that we are anxious, depressed, or disappointed, an opportunity opens. Then just two things are required: to start practicing and to keep going.

While many people come to meditation to feel better, in time the spiritual nature of the practice emerges. I am going to go out on a limb (I hear this is where the fruit is) to say this is because our lives are spiritual paths, and the practice is one that guides each of us to look at our lives. You will find that it does not contradict any faiths, nor propose any belief systems.

Consider, what would there be-- who would we be-- if stress were ended?

I have been inspired to write and illustrate this book out of the ever-increasing happiness and peace in my life and a great enthusiasm to share it, particularly with incarcerated men and women. I have been teaching in detention centers since 2009. Service work is a good testing ground for these ideas, and my confidence in them is great.

I encourage you to take your time. This is an exploration. Give yourself permission to pause, check in often with how you are feeling, and verify! Finally, feel free to create and invent your own testing methods.

How to Meditate, and Why

We meditate to end stress and suffering.

We all feel it: from the everyday irritations to life-shattering disappointments and difficulties. We all share common desires for happiness, safety, and peace that are never satisfied--at least not for long. When our relationships, health, or jobs are not going right, we feel anxious and uneasy. Mindfulness is an effective cure for stress, and meditation is a way to develop mindfulness.

We know we want to be happy and at peace, but we might have a dull and weary feeling that it isn't possible. We can start by noticing what we *are* doing anyway: how much time we spend planning, fixing, blaming, trying harder, escaping, or soothing ourselves. Then we might begin to clue into to the fact that, whatever our particular go-to strategy is, it isn't *actually working*. But--this is good news! Despair makes way for a willingness to abandon the old ways.

How do we understand stress and suffering? If we can find the cause, can we eliminate it?

There is one THING that, when cultivated and regularly practiced, leads TO DEEP Spiritual intention TO PEACE, to mindfulness, and clear comprehension, TO VISION and KNOWLEDGE, to a happy life here and NOW; and to the culmination of wisdom and awakening. And what is that one Thing? It is mindfulness centered on the BODY.

Siddhartha Gautama

Right now, Take Five: just count five breaths. What do you notice? What is the feeling? Is there anxiety? Boredom? What about in the body? Is there tension? Where? Jaw? Shoulders? Belly? And in the mind? Any images? Can you notice an attitude or mood?

This is the foundation of meditation (that we will practice again and again): sitting still, turning our attention inward, making our present moment experience--no matter what it is--the place where we look for the answers we seek.

This is not to say that sitting still and noticing is fun or easy. It often isn't. When we first try meditating, we see that our thoughts don't stop, they wander around, and we may feel tense and effortful. Our bodies may feel agitated and we can't sit still. But this not-fun-confused-uneasy-tight-muscled experience is the teacher, so ... we learn to *pay attention* to it. This alone is really different from the old way.

To develop this foundation we choose something in the present moment on which to anchor our attention, for example, the breath as it moves our bodies. At first, we might be able to focus on the breath for only a couple of seconds before we lose focus and we find ourselves lost in thought. That's OK, this is how it works. We start to understand the mind by observing what it does *instead* of following the breath.

Soon we begin to see some really interesting things! Not only are the answers within, but the cause of stress is within. And this is different from what we thought. It isn't that we lost our job or are separated from our loved ones, but it is something about our way of holding and responding to the experience that is the culprit. After all, only *we* clench our jaws, tense our shoulders, or grip our hands. All the tension is in the muscles that we consciously or unconsciously move. Our bodies reflect the way our minds are grasping-- restlessly--problematically-- at something that cannot be grasped: life in constant change.

Mindfulness is no small task, but bit by bit and over time, the practice disassembles stress. No one can do this for us, however. We need to rally the courage and the energy by making a commitment to our happiness and peace—even five conscious breaths a day is good.

PRACTICE: Take Five 1. Sit still. 2. Notice. 3. Take five breaths. 4. Notice

Recognizing-- pausing, naming, and noticing stress when we are feeling it, is a key part of this practice. You might begin to ask yourself: how briefly do I feel dissatisfaction, anxiety, and unhappiness? How automatically do I try to stop those feelings?

It might seem counterintuitive, but the recognition of stress and suffering is the first step toward easing it. Otherwise, we feel the unease, but not for long: soon we're skittering off into our habitual schemes to get rid of it. *Our training in mindfulness begins by pausing with the bare acknowledgment of our unease.*

This recognition is so important, because it turns our life in another direction—away from resistance to our feelings, and toward freedom. This sounds simple, but it isn't easy. We don't want to admit that we're struggling and suffering, again. Yet, the freedom is in recognizing this again and again. The more we see it, the better!

The Cause

How can we understand the cause of our unhappiness? Our usual method is trying to figure it out. Instead, try directly observing what is felt within the body, using the movement of the breath. You might think of this as 'home plate.' The instruction is to stay with the feeling of the breath as continuously as possible-- this alone has a calming effect. But it often happens, for example, that we suddenly want to jump up and get something to eat. We might discover that our jaws are clenched, or that there's an uneasy feeling in our legs. What happened?

Something happened, and we missed it. So, we go back to 'home plate' and again watch the breath. Here something comes again, yet this time, we're paying closer attention and notice that maybe an uncomfortable feeling or emotion has flickered by. What was that?

We didn't quite catch it, so back 'home' we go. This time, we notice how the mind is commenting on our experience. It might be saying something like, "This isn't working." Or, we might notice that we want to move in order to feel better. And then we see that with those thoughts, an uncomfortable feeling arises and we want to jump up and get something to eat.

Understanding how the mind works is a long process with many, many facets. Yet each time we return 'home' to the present moment, we've seen a little more of the way the mind works, and in the seeing of it, *we emancipate ourselves a little more.*

From the home plate of the present moment, we can begin to notice that our usual response to unease is WANTING. Our unease feels bad, so we want things that feel good. Not only that, but we also want our way and we want to be in control. We want to get rid of things: back pain, worry, or certain people. And we want to be entertained, changing the channel on everything just to escape boredom! This wanting can be called grasping or craving. If we continue in this direction (and most everyone else is doing this, so we feel normal) we can get very used to our cravings. In time, we become attached and even stuck to what we think will fix our unhappiness. Another way to say it is that we are addicted.

When we just recognize the unease, we start to see how we participate in it. Then we understand that ending this dissatisfaction is possible. Up to now, we simply didn't know: Getting what we want doesn't end stress and suffering! What! Yet the more we recognize this, again and again, the more we're willing and able to let go of our of our old way.

The Cure

Our spiritual path is to consciously let go--beginning with the tension in the body-- while at the same time paying close attention to our experience in this precise moment.

Our spiritual practice is both a relaxing and a waking up.

The Path

There are many ways of addicting, and many ways of letting go. We can practice mindfulness in daily life, we can develop mindfulness by meditating regularly, and we can clarify our direction by the insights that naturally arise with this practice. The path is not so much a sequence of steps to take in order, but rather qualities to look for and develop. Developing each quality builds on all the others.

The word 'right' can mean many things.
Here, it is meant in the way a boat can be tipping too far one way, and then it is righted.

Right Understanding

Right dNTentioN

Right Speech

right action

RightWork

RIGhT Effort

RIGhT mindfulNeSS

riGhT concentration

Right nderstanding

"I don't want the peace that passeth understanding, I want the understanding which bringeth peace."
-Helen Keller

We do need some conceptual understanding of the ideas, but the real understanding comes from recognizing, again and again, the unease and stress in the body. The habits of mind leave an imprint in the body of the many ways 'I want.' Once we understand that, *we can decide to end it.* Finally, we begin our practice, experimenting and testing the many ways of doing this.

Rather than trying to get rid of our unease, we turn to it. From observation we understand how it happens. A willingness begins in us to see all the ways we take part in our unease and stress and unhappiness. Sometimes slowly, sometimes dramatically, we let them go.

Right ntention

"If you don't know where you are going you are going to end up where you are headed."
-Old Chinese Proverb

To simplify, there are two kinds of intentions, and two kinds of thoughts that nurture those intentions; one kind results in unhappiness, and the other results in happiness. With mindfulness, we can begin to live more intentionally. We can decide to be happy and at ease.

Thoughts concerned with self-centered wanting and getting of any kind: wanting money, status, pleasure, even wanting spiritual achievements; thoughts that arise out of fear, anger and irritation; and thoughts of getting rid of or revenge all lead to unhappiness. The opposite thoughts: letting go of self-centered wanting, generosity, kindness, compassion, good-will, helpfulness, and non-harming, for ourselves and others, lead to happiness.

Practice: Exhale completely. Inhale to extend the spine, and leaving the spine extended, relax on the exhale. First notice whatever tension is present in the body. Consciously relax that. Pause, then notice, again, whatever tension is present, and relax that. Continue in this way, looking for deeper layers of tension that can be brought to consciousness. Is there any limit to letting go?

GUIDE YOURSELF
to
LIVING

IN
HARMONY

Through care of speech, action, and work

Right Speech,  Action, Work

"…all beings are the owner of their actions, heir to their actions, born of their actions, related through their actions, and live dependent on their actions. Whatever they do, for good or for evil, to that will they fall heir." - Anguttara Nikaya 5.57

"All happiness comes from the desire for others to be happy. All misery comes from the desire for oneself to be happy." - Shantideva

"Love your neighbor as yourself." - Leviticus 19:18

Intentions that lead to happiness do so because we let go, bit by bit or all at once, of our self-centered strategy. If we are letting go of that, we are making room in our hearts and minds for other people, other living beings, and the world around us.

Soon, it becomes obvious how much this matters! We are all interconnected and our actions truly have an effect on our world.

Our speech can be an area of suffering and therefore a great place for practicing mindfulness. We can notice, for instance, how we joke. Is everyone laughing? Are my jokes at someone's expense, even my own? We can notice how we want to be seen when we speak, or if we're speaking to get something, or to get back at someone, or to hear ourselves speak, or to show how much we know, or to be liked or respected or feared. We can ask: does this bring me to lasting peace and happiness? What happens if I just say nothing?

Our 'small' actions matter, too. How do we move in a group, stack the chairs, or walk across the room? Am I washing the dishes with attention or am I trying to skip past this to get to the next thing? What about driving? After I yell at another driver, am I happier? I might have a temporary feeling of power, but is there lasting happiness?

There's no need to go to a special quiet place like a mountain top or a deserted beach: a noisy kitchen or cell-block can give us on-the-job training in mindfulness. A very simple yet powerful way to begin is to *pay attention* to sounds.

We can practice at work by asking 'How can I help?' as we let go of 'What's in it for me?'

PRACTICE: Say something kind and watch what happens.
PRACTICE: Become aware of 'inter-being' by making a list of all the people, animals, plants, and elements that went into your last meal.

MINDFULNESS

Open Quiet
Alert Present

Right  Mindfulness

"It's like this." -Ajahn Sumedho

Mindfulness is paying attention, intentionally, to what is here and now, in other words, to reality. It may be hard to say what reality is, but it can be *directly known* though our senses. Directly knowing reality is so obvious that we miss it!

Mindfulness is a particular skill. It is an observation of everything, rather than the normal habit of believing everything we think about how things should be and reacting because they are not. By sitting still and putting our attention on the breath, over and over, we gradually educate the mind to stay present, and flow like the breath. Thoughts are allowed to come and go, so their demands are less convincing. We begin to see what's what: what is a thought, and what is reality.

The fact is, nothing can exist at any other time than the present. It's all we get. Our sensations and emotions are happening in the present moment, as are our thoughts. But in thought, we create images and stories of the future, the past, or a mixture of the two: reviewing the past and redoing it in the future! We also create rules and beliefs, and it can feel very much like watching a movie, but with the added special effects of tension in the body. With these special effects, our thought-movies can seem really believable, invoking fantasies of something 'better,' or showing reruns of past horrors. And we love horror movies! Hit the repeat button!

Whichever movie happens to be playing in our head, it's not what is happening now. And yet we think we need these mental movies. We lay them over our sensible reality. When we do this, our awareness of reality becomes dimmed and even distorted, and we end up feeling confused and stressed.

The present moment is a place to rest the attention that is reliable. It is always exactly as it is.

Practice: Relax the body and come into stillness. Name what is present. Pause and breathe gently. What is happening now? Name that, pause and breathe gently. Continue in this way.

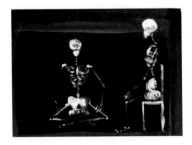

*in meditation
sit with hips
higher
than knees*

Right  Concentration

"There is no concentration without wisdom, no wisdom without concentration. One who has both concentration and wisdom is close to peace and emancipation." – Bhante Gunaratana

Concentration is a kind of meditation used to train the mind to slow down and focus. Any meditation that points the attention on a single, present-moment object like sound, the breath, or a feeling in the body, is a concentration meditation. (Mantras and prayer are examples of concentration meditations) The object serves as an anchor. When *we notice* the mind has left the anchor, creating imaginary conversations or reviewing memories or plans, a little chink in our habit is made. And thankfully so, we are waking up to reality! No need to undo anything, no need to remember any rules or steps to the present moment. Immediately, we can drop into it. It is always right here!

The root of the word 'spirit' is *spirare*, which means 'to breathe.' So we can say that, by following the breath, we let the spirit guide us.

Concentrate
to bring to, or direct to, a common center;
to unite more closely;
To to Gather into one body;
increase Strength by
Removing diluting material;
to fix exclusive attention on

Concentration meditation helps 'monkey mind,' that state of mind that swings from thing to thing to thing....

a body map to aid concentration

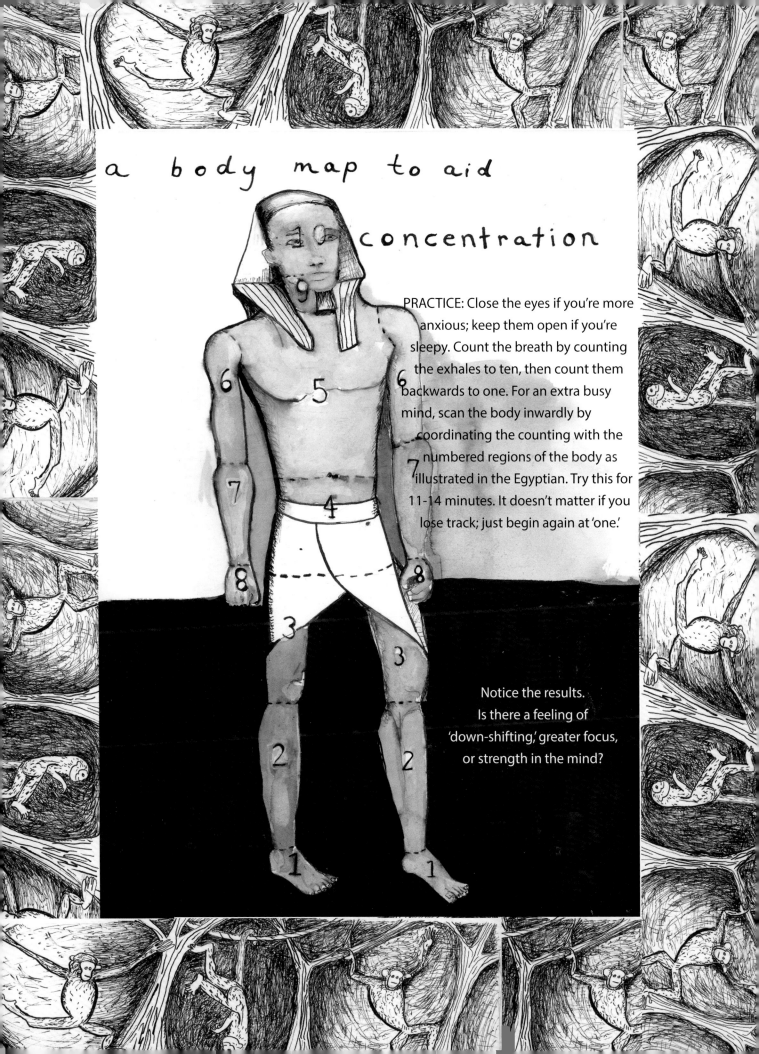

PRACTICE: Close the eyes if you're more anxious; keep them open if you're sleepy. Count the breath by counting the exhales to ten, then count them backwards to one. For an extra busy mind, scan the body inwardly by coordinating the counting with the numbered regions of the body as illustrated in the Egyptian. Try this for 11-14 minutes. It doesn't matter if you lose track; just begin again at 'one.'

Notice the results.
Is there a feeling of
'down-shifting,' greater focus,
or strength in the mind?

Right  Effort

"Difficult to detect and very subtle, the mind seizes whatever it wants; so let a wise one guard one's mind, for a guarded mind brings happiness." - Dhammapada 3:36

As the mind and body settle, we mindfully observe our present-moment experience. Soon, we are able to encourage thoughts that are kind and helpful, and guard against those that aren't. As we begin to see the benefits-- no longer harming ourselves or others and more peace and happiness-- we are inspired to practice both meditation and mindfulness in speech, action, and work.

At the same time, we let go of:

> *wanting to be right,*
> *wanting to know,*
> *wanting to look good,*
> *wanting security,*
> *wanting to be seen*
> *as a good person* or
> A HARD WORKER,
> *wanting to be more spiritual,*
> *wanting to be the*
> *most miserable,*
> *wanting more, less,*
> *or different*

… to name just a few of the popular ones.

Even as we make this deep commitment, what often happens is that we meet with great resistance, and inwardly go to war with our experience. We may want to meditate every day, and then some lazy, bored feeling takes over. Or we meditate with a grim determination. Our old habits of mind do not want to let go!

In the practice of meditation, notice whenever intention and attention becomes *either* lazy or strained. Right effort is an ongoing balancing act of relaxing AND waking up.

Not too loose

Not too tight

Not too loose

Not too tight

Not too loose

Compassion

Now here is a very important thing. In aiming our intentions to happiness, ease, and peace, we notice the way we are *holding ourselves*. What is our attitude to ourselves, our experience? Simple attention can soften the tension in the body- we really need attention. Remember this moment, no matter what, is our human condition.

When we check in with ourselves, though, we often discover the inner critic: a harsh and unkind attitude toward our mistakes, our disconnection from others, our appearance, our accomplishments, and more. We might believe that we need more 'discipline' to be better, and beat up on ourselves. Does that ever work?

Compassion means 'to suffer with.' We don't resist our feelings. Instead, we just allow ourselves to be with the suffering, letting up on how we're holding ourselves. In other words, we cradle our 'inner baby' - we don't hit the baby!

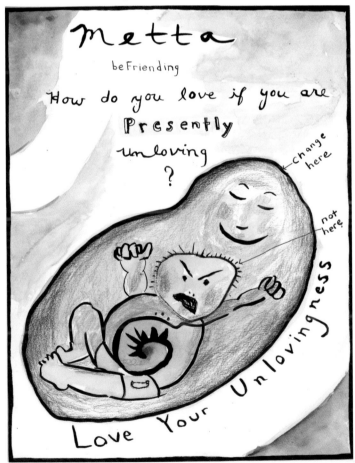

There is no limit to the amount of compassion we can offer ourselves and others. We don't need to earn or 'deserve' compassion. In fact, the more painful the trouble, the more compassion is called for. As we practice self-compassion, notice how compassion for others naturally increases, and how much easier it is to do right and be kind.

Recognizing the voice of the inner critic is recognizing our old habits of mind that we learned, our conditioning. That voice in our head is what we as children heard our parents or caregivers saying. Seeing this is a big step in understanding it is not the authority today. The messages can be very subtle and difficult to detect, but we feel them in the body as a sense of contraction, or a blocking, or a pressing down; or in our feelings as a belittling; or in our thoughts as 'not good,' 'not right,' or 'not enough.' The inner critic uses comparison and judgment, and takes us away from the present into thoughts of an ideal world--a promise that it never keeps.

It is healthy to be alert to, name, and guard against the inner critic.

PRACTICE: While sitting in meditation or anytime throughout the day, notice which thoughts are helpful, and which ones are not.

Tonglen, which means 'giving and receiving,' is a very simple but counterintuitive breathing practice. In tonglen, we breathe **in** stress, anger, and anxiety; the troubling news of the world; all those things we might normally run like mad to get away from. Then, we breathe out the opposite: peace, fearlessness, happiness. With the inhale, we touch the trouble. With the exhale, we imagine these good things for ourselves, and for others who, right now, are feeling the same things we feel.

I Begin by offering kindness to the self.

PRACTICE: In meditation, try these phrases "May I be happy, may I be safe, may I be strong, may I be at ease." Then try bringing other people to mind: "May you be happy, may you be safe, may you be strong, may you be at ease."
Notice when you have a negative reaction to these phrases.
See if you can hold your negative reaction with kindness.

 eelings

"What we resist persists." -Carl Jung

Feelings-- just the basic 'pleasant' and 'unpleasant' responses--link sensations in the body to thinking. Our runaway habits and addictions that come from trying to increase, maintain, or repeat pleasant feelings and trying to make unpleasant feelings go away, can be dis-empowered by breaking the link with mindfulness of what we're feeling. Simply noticing 'pleasant' and 'unpleasant,' is a powerful but effortless interruption of habitual reactions and addictions.

Other than the stories that we invent, what else is there? And, notice how often our stories are *the cause* of our 'unpleasant' feelings.

Emotions result from the stories and thoughts about what is pleasant and unpleasant. As we are experiencing 'emotion-thoughts', we can take time to look for the *exact word or phrase* that names the experience, rejecting the first or second choice if we find it isn't quite right. This is checking for resonance. Once we've found the right word, we can pause for a moment and feel what we feel. We can give it space, so to speak, allowing it to move if it wants to move.

When working with difficult emotions, you might try thanking them, which is another way to let go of resistance, and to feel inwardly connected. They are our feelings, after all!

tight   excited   sad jealous
alert   open   irritated   loving
anxious curious lost relaxed
engaged shaky confused
angry   inspired

PRACTICE: Scan the body. Allow a 'felt sense' to develop.
Pause, and let it be: pleasant, unpleasant, or neutral.
What does it need?

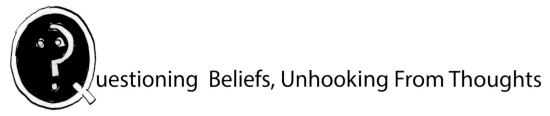

Questioning Beliefs, Unhooking From Thoughts

"Who would you be without your story?" - Byron Katie

"Do not seek the truth, only cease to cherish opinions." - Seng T'san

"For as he thinketh in his heart, so is he." - Proverbs 23:7

"Don't believe everything you think." - AA Wisdom

Many people expect meditation to stop the thoughts. So we *suspect* that our stress is in our thinking even if at the same time we believe that situations are happening **to us**-- that *they* are the problem and we need to fix them.

We really worry, trying out different solutions, often talking to other people looking for agreement. When we are hurting and in the middle of a problem, it is hard to see: questioning our beliefs is more important than fixing the problem 'out there.'

Begin with asking, "What am I believing?" Then kindly pay attention to the body and follow with the bare acknowledgment that 'there is stress.' Notice what the feeling is underlying it all. It is likely an unpleasant feeling like fear or a compulsive feeling like desire. Keeping the feelings going are things we believe about how we are supposed to be or how you are supposed to be or how life is supposed to be. Mindfulness unhooks us from our thoughts because we are observing the thoughts, but not necessarily believing them. This is called dis-identifying.

Find that thought that causes the belly to tighten. For example, 'Its always like this.' 'People are so ignorant.' 'I need to do more.' Repeat the thought to yourself and ask, 'Is this what I think?' Then ask 'Is it true?'

Thoughts that start with 'I need…' 'I should…' 'They should…' or that contain 'always' or 'never' and end with a lot of tension and stress are good to investigate. If our beliefs are going to cause so much stress, it might be worth it to find out if they are true!

While sitting in meditation, pause from time to time and simply note, 'oh, thinking.' Or label the thoughts 'planning,' 'regretting,' 'inner critic,' or repeat the thoughts back to yourself. 'This is stupid.'

Notice the image of yourself that you create in your thoughts. What are you believing about how you should be? When you notice a thought that feels very stressful, see if you can see a 'you,' a self-image, in the story you are creating, sometimes center stage, sometimes off to one side.

These self-images, these ideas of 'I' and all the shoulds about life, are the ego. The voice of the inner critic keeps it going, beating us up to keep us in line. This self-imaging was learned when we were young. The ego is our childlike self, who attempts to make our experience solid and predictable so that we can know how to safely proceed. So allow the natural compassion to yourself that you would feel for any suffering child. If we ignore or beat up on our childlike patterns, they really stay with us.

Byron Katie developed an effective system, four questions and a turnaround, that can dis-empower any stressful thought.

It really helps to write down the answers.

1. Is it true?
2. Can I absolutely know that it is true?
3. What happens when I think this?
4. Who would I be without this thought?
Turnaround: Is the exact opposite as true or truer?

FIVE REMEMBRANCES

I am of a nature to grow old.
There is no way to escape growing old.

I am of a nature to have ill health
There is no way to escape having ill health.

I am of a nature to die.
There is no way to escape death.

All that is dear to me
and everyone I love
are of the nature to change.
There is no way to escape being
separated from them.

My actions are my only
true belongings
I cannot escape the consequences
of my actions.

My actions are the ground on
which I stand.

-upajjhatthana sutta

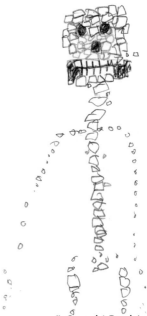

Impermanence

"Don't cry because it's over; smile because it happened." - Dr. Seuss

"Renunciation is not giving up the things of this world, but accepting that they go away"- Suzuki Roshi

We know that nothing lasts. We don't want to know this. It seems like bad news. So, we tend to think and behave in denial of this plain truth. We might notice how many things we do to remain in denial. Just watch TV. Advertisements are very revealing of this human misdirection. Are we purchasing Forever with "A Diamond is Forever"?

Yet, if we can allow ourselves to look at and remember the truth of impermanence, we can find a surprising freedom. Consider: what would happen to our fears about our relationships, health, or finances if we continued to remember, moment to moment, that everything that arises also passes away? We might fear, for example, that if we start crying we will never stop, but mind states and feelings also arise and pass away.

In remembering that nothing lasts, we can be more present. More and more, resting our attention on the breath, letting go of all we hold so tightly, we can come to deeply appreciate nature, people, creatures, seasons, planets, stars, right now, in this exact moment, and all the quiet mystery that is always here.

PRACTICE: Sense into what you notice around you, and become aware of what changes, moment to moment.

PRACTICE: The next time you watch TV, notice when the messages in the commercials promise anything secure and permanent.

Community

The obstacles to our meditation and mindfulness practice can feel overwhelming: our habitual, fruitless drives for pleasure and security; our constant anxiety and doubt about how we're doing or how things are going; and the deep exhaustion that can occur as we slow down to practice. So often, the mind doesn't want to do it!

It can be helpful to find or create a group to meditate with. If you're willing to be honest and, when possible, let go of any need to control, or to be seen in a certain way, connecting with a community of others interested in mindfulness can support you when facing the resistance and obstacles to practice.

In a group we may find more experienced meditators, who might offer advice if needed. We might also find less experienced meditators and be able to offer the kind of support that experience provides. Out of the atmosphere of mutuality and shared connection grows a field of strength that all can beneficially draw on.

When we meditate with others we come to see that our stresses, anxieties, difficulties and suffering are not as unique as we may think they are when we are alone and in the middle of them. When we practice with others we might see how our suffering comes from being human, and how we share and belong in this human family. We are truly not alone.

Many communities of mindfulness practitioners exist today, as do free books(accesstoinsight.org) and talks (dharmaseed.org) on the Internet. Yet, community can also be as simple as two or three people getting together regularly to sit and to talk about these ideas.

Service

Keep in mind our simple objective: ending suffering. Self-centered desires are the cause of suffering. A generosity practice of service to others takes the self out of the center.

How can I be of service? How isn't always obvious, so let the question circulate in your heart.

Intentions matter. When I teach in the detention centers, I notice intentions that keep me focused on myself-- wanting to be heard, trying to get it right. Then, if possible, I extend compassion to the suffering that results from those self-centered desires.

I also notice intentions that shift the focus away from me such as listening, letting my heart be open, and being kind, lead to a lasting happiness.

May The Long Time Sun
Shine Upon You
All Love Surround You
And The Pure Light
Within You
Guide Your Way On